A GUIDE FOR

YOUNG BATTERS
& BASERUNNERS

ALSO BY DON OSTER

A Guide for Young Pitchers
with Bill McMillan

A Guide for Young Softball Pitchers
with Jacque Hunter

All from The Lyons Press

A GUIDE FOR
YOUNG BATTERS
& BASERUNNERS

Don Oster and Bill McMillan

j 796.35
7 05

THE LYONS PRESS
GUILFORD, CONNECTICUT
An imprint of The Globe Pequot Press

The Lyons Press is an imprint of The Globe Pequot Press.

10 9 8 7 6 5 4 3 2 1

Printed in the United States of America

Library of Congress Cataloging-in-Publication Data

Oster, Don.
   A Young player's guide to hitting, bunting, and baserunning / by Don
   Oster and Bill McMillan.
      p. cm.
   ISBN 1-59228-688-7 (trade paper)
Baseball — Offense. 2. Batting (Baseball) I. McMillan, Bill, 1944– II. Title.

GV867.7.O78 2004
796.357'26 — dc22

               2004065027

CONTENTS

ACKNOWLEDGMENTS

This is to recognize the contributions of the hundreds of players and coaches Bill and I have worked with during many years of coaching youth baseball. It was a teaching and learning experience that went both ways. Some of the most successful years were not measured in wins and losses but in the improvement of teams through tough seasons.

We also owe thanks to our sons, Mike and Dave McMillan and Mark Oster, who played, then lured us into coaching. And special thanks to our wives, who supported us through long seasons followed by annual family vacations at postseason tournaments in not exactly garden spots.

An exceptional team of youngsters carried me as a manager to the Little League World Series in 1985. I will forever be in their debt for the experience of a lifetime.

ACKNOWLEDGMENTS

And finally, thanks to the New Albany, Indiana, Township Little League Organization, where the photos were taken for this book. Special thanks to Tony and Matt Kremer, Steve and Josh Santana, and Diane Carter and Nathan Prater for their assistance in the photo process.

Don Oster

A GUIDE FOR
YOUNG BATTERS
& BASERUNNERS

INTRODUCTION

Batting is fun. Unlike some other baseball fundamentals, it's even fun to practice. Very few things compare to the feel of a solid hit and the sight of a line drive rocketing toward the outfield grass. Batting is not easy. You are trying to solidly hit a round object (the ball) with another round object (the bat). But, once you learn the fundamentals and work hard at practicing them, you can become a good hitter.

Hitting is what the first part of this book is all about. First you will learn batting fundamentals and then several practice drills to help you improve your skills. This book is not about hitting home runs. Those will come in time, usually when you least expect them. Your baseball career is just starting. Sound batting fundamentals will serve you well throughout your career. By following the basics you will become a good contact hitter. If you're making good, solid contact with the pitches, the base hits will fall.

Hitting can be frustrating because the best batters at all levels only get it right between three and four times out of each ten official at bats. There will be times when it seems that each ball you hit well is hit directly at a fielder. But you must keep your confidence and stick with the basics. Always remember that if you're making good contact you will be a successful batter in the long run.

Hitting isn't all there is to the offensive part of the game. There are other skills to learn that can help you become a total offensive player. Success at the plate isn't always about ripping line drives. Baseball is a team game. Every player on a team must be able to bunt. Sometimes a simple little bunt can be a game breaker. You will learn bunting basics, including sacrifice bunts and bunts for base hits.

Next, we go into game situations where you learn what to look for before you go to bat. We discuss things like sizing up the pitcher, knowing the game situation, and your job when you are the on-deck batter. Then we cover how to hit with a purpose. This includes ways to work a pitcher during an at bat and how to adjust to get the most out of each time at the plate.

You must score to win ball games. Good baserunning can win games, and baserunning errors can cause losses. We tell you how to become a smart base runner. While your base coaches direct much of the baserunning, you also have responsibilities. These responsibilities include having your head in the game and knowing what to look for and how to react.

The next chapter sums up individual and team aspects of the game. In this chapter, you will learn strategies for advancing runners and the characteristics of a good offensive team.

A chapter on the hitter's attitude suggests how a good hitter should approach each at bat with a positive "can-do" attitude. Believing in yourself and trusting your swing are characteristics that will help you be a good hitter.

In the final chapter, Common Batting Faults, mistakes that reduce a hitter's effectiveness are described. These are departures from good hitting fundamentals that batters should avoid. Once one of these flaws is recognized, it must be corrected.

Use the basics, practice hard, and learn from any mistakes. You're on the way to a lot of fun during a successful baseball career.

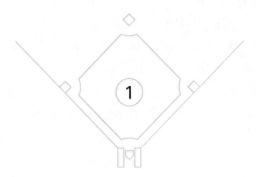

THE SOLID HITTER

The batter is on deck. He's swinging a weighted bat to warm up. His swings aren't hard. They are just quick enough to loosen his arms and shoulders. While he takes the swings, he's studying the pitcher.

The pitcher throws three-quarter overhand with a fairly smooth motion. He seems to be throwing rather hard and most of the pitches are strikes. Once in a while the pitcher tries to throw some sort of curveball. It looks like a spinner, doesn't break a lot, and shouldn't be a problem to hit. The pitcher also throws a change-up. The batter looks for a difference in the pitcher's motion that will give away a curve or change-up, but if the pitcher is good, there doesn't seem to be a change in his motion on any pitches. The hitter knows he'll look first for the fastball and adjust if a different pitch is thrown.

Before going to the plate, he will pick up his regular bat and swing it a few times. His swing is quick, tight, and compact. His teammate's turn at bat is over. He knows the game situation. He knows the number of outs and if there are runners on base. As he approaches the plate, he looks at the positions of the first and third basemen. If either fielder is playing back, that might be a good place for a bunt. When he reaches the batter's box he uses his toe to smooth the dirt where he will take his stance. He wants a good, firm base for his feet to stride and hit. He looks at the third-base coach for a signal. Whatever the coach wants, the confident batter can do. He can bunt or fake bunt. He can take a pitch or hit away. He can execute. This batter has his head in the game.

As he takes his position in the batter's box, his feet are a little more than shoulder width apart, and he is balanced on the balls of his feet with a little more weight on his back leg. His knees and waist are bent slightly. He reaches out with his bat to make sure he can reach a pitch on the outside corner of the plate. The batter takes a couple of half swings, and moves into his stance. His head is solid. His eyes are level and focused on the pitcher.

This batter knows the strike zone. He sees it as an imaginary window in front of the plate. It is as wide as the plate and extends from the top of his knees to the letters on his uniform. The pitcher will be trying to throw a strike through this area. From his drills and batting practice, the batter has confidence that he can make solid contact with a pitch in the window most of the time. He can pull inside pitches and take outside pitches to the opposite field. Knowing the strike zone as well as he does, the batter doesn't often help the pitcher by swinging at bad pitches. He almost never takes a called third strike because he knows there are pitches "too close to take." He will swing to guard the plate when there is a two-strike count. This is a confident batter.

The batter knows stress or tension can be his enemy. No matter how tight the game situation becomes, he doesn't let stress or nerves become a problem when he's batting. If he feels tense, he will ask the umpire for time out and step out of the box. Taking a couple of deep breaths in this situation should help relieve any nervous tension he feels. This batter has good self-control.

If the coach doesn't ask for a sacrifice bunt to advance base runners, the batter's prime objective is to get on base. He wants to hit his way on base, but he knows this won't happen more than three or four times out of ten at bats. He can contact any pitch in the strike zone. The batter will work the count looking for a pitch to hit, and make adjustments to the pitcher's speed as necessary. He isn't too proud to take base on balls. If the pitcher doesn't give him a pitch to hit, he'll certainly take the free pass and a chance to score. This is a controlled, aggressive batter who is ready to make a contribution to his team.

A batter with these attributes, who has learned and practiced sound batting fundamentals, will become a successful hitter.

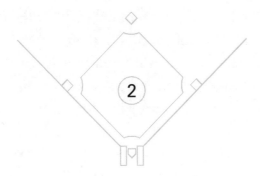

THE FUNDAMENTALS
OF HITTING

Hitting is about timing. It is about getting your body in the proper position to time the pitch. How the parts of your body work together in hitting a baseball is called the mechanics of hitting. You must have good mechanics to be a good, consistent hitter. Learn and practice good mechanics. The picture sequence (below) shows a young hitter who has good hitting mechanics.

THE BASICS

Regardless of how you are built, practicing some basics can make you a better hitter.

- Stay balanced through the entire hitting motion. Keep your body solid and under control.
- Eliminate wasted motion. Be smooth and powerful. Maintain a smooth tempo.
- Be relaxed and as tension-free as possible. If your hands, legs, and shoulders are tight, your muscle movements will be tight, and your swing will not be smooth.
- Always keep your eyes on the ball. Watch it in the pitcher's hand. Try to watch it hit the bat. If you can't swing at the pitch, watch it all the way to the catcher's glove.

Ready.

Stride.

Initiate swing.

Contact.

Follow-through.

- Keep your head steady and down through the swing.
- Have a short, compact swing. This kind of swing will allow you to make more consistent contact with the ball and hit a lot of hard line drives.
- Avoid a big, loopy swing. The loopy swing takes longer to get the bat to the ball and will hurt your consistency and bat speed.
- Be aggressive at going after the ball. Don't swing at bad pitches, but don't go to the plate looking for a walk. If you don't plan to use the bat, don't take it with you to the plate.
- Hit through the ball, not to it. Don't slow down your swing at contact. Try to drive your bat right through the middle of the ball.

BAT SELECTION

Picking the right bat is an important part of being a good hitter. Young players often choose bats that are too long or too heavy. You want a bat that will give you good bat speed in your swing. Find a short, light bat that you can handle. A good way to find out if a bat is too heavy for you is to hold it straight out in front of you, with one hand, at shoulder height. If you can't hold it for thirty seconds, the bat is too heavy.

Most modern metal bats have large barrels. You'll have a lot of hitting surface even with a small bat. The thickness of the bat handle is a matter of personal preference. Pick one that feels good in your hands.

THE GRIP

The bat should feel comfortable in your hands. The grip should be as loose as it can be and let you control the bat through the swing. Squeezing the bat too tightly is often called "the white knuckle grip." This grip creates tension and reduces flexibility in your wrists. Ideally, the bat should be gripped in the middle joint of the fingers of both hands. Most young players will need to grip the bat more in the palms of their hands.

THE STANCE

How you set yourself in the batter's box affects how well you can hit. Pay special attention to the following characteristics of a good stance.

Foot Placement

Your feet should be parallel and a little more than a shoulder width apart. Your front shoulder should be pointing at the pitcher. This is called a square stance. Some hitters will place their front foot behind their back foot (open stance). Others will place their front foot in front of the back foot (closed stance). It is best to use a square stance because, regardless where they start, good hitters end up stepping directly toward the pitcher. The open and closed stances cause wasted motion and can affect balance.

Body Posture

You should be bent slightly forward at the waist, and your knees should be slightly bent. Your weight should be on the balls, not the heels, of your feet. This position sets a foundation that is balanced and flexible.

Hands and Bat Position

To get the most compact swing, your hands should be at the armpit of your back shoulder with your top hand at about shoulder height. Your bat should be at a forty-five-degree angle with the ground. This is a solid hitting position. Hitters who hold their hands high, hold the bat straight up, or lay it straight behind them must adjust their swings to get their hands and bat into a solid position. Start in a solid position. You will have a more fluid, consistent swing.

As you get older, you might want to move your hands back in line with your back shoulder or maybe even farther back. This will cause your front shoulder to

turn inward. If you can make consistent contact with the ball this way, you should have more power.

When you are in your stance, you should have some slight movement in your hands. Timing to hit the ball starts with using your hands to time the rhythm of the pitcher's delivery.

Head Position

Your head should be fully facing the pitcher and your eyes should be focused on the ball.

Position in the Batter's Box

Where you stand in the batter's box will be greatly affected by the way you are built, the length of your arms and legs, and so on. Your position in the batter's box should let you do two things:

- You should be able to cover the outside part of the plate when your arms are fully extended during the swing.
- You should be able to hit the ball in front of the plate.

If you have short arms, you will need to stand closer to the plate and closer to the front of the batter's box than if you are tall and have long arms.

HITTING

The 60/40 Rule

Hitting is a continuous motion. When you hit, your weight shifts from your back foot to the front foot and your hips open to face the pitcher. When you are in your stance, 60 percent of your weight should be on your back foot and 40 percent should be on your front foot. When you contact the ball, you should have 60 percent of your weight on your front foot and only 40 percent on your back foot. Following this rule will help you have a balanced, compact swing. Take one or two half swings in the batter's box to establish a 60/40 tempo.

The Stride

A common baseball expression is "stride to hit." This expression means that the first thing that happens during the swing is the stride. Take a short, comfortable stride toward the pitcher with your front foot. Do not point your toes at the pitcher. Your feet should stay parallel. You are now on perfect balance with 50 percent of your weight on each foot.

The Ready Position

After your stride, your head stays solid, and your hands are back and at armpit level. Your hips have not started to turn. Now you should see why your hands should be at the armpits in your stance. It is because you waste no motion in getting them where they belong in the ready position. Even if you think that you can hold your hands farther back in your stance, they need to get to where they belong in the ready position.

The Swing

As your weight and your hips begin to turn, your hands move forward. Notice that the hands and the knob of the bat lead the swing through the strike zone.

The Contact Position

It is now time to attack the ball. Your weight shift is complete. You use both hands to throw the barrel of the bat at the center of the ball. Your arms begin to extend. When you contact the ball, your arms should be fully extended. Hit the ball in front of the plate.

The Follow-Through

A good follow-through lets you hit through the ball and drive it hard. During the follow-through you continue to pull through the ball with your arms, your hands, and the

barrel of the bat. Most good hitters finish the follow-through facing the pitcher and have the toes of their back foot pointed toward the ground.

CLEANING UP

Some additional fundamentals are worth remembering.

Not Taking One for the Club

As a young player, it's perfectly natural to be a little afraid when you first start hitting. There are some specific things that you can do to help you avoid getting hit by a pitch.

- Have a balanced and relaxed stance like the one we talked about earlier. Do not be in a rigid, locked position. If you are rigid, you will not be able to move out of the way of the ball.
- If you think you are going to be hit, "roll away from the ball." This involves turning your upper body toward the catcher and lowering your head. Your feet do not need to move. This is a good way to protect your head and upper body.
- It is a good idea to practice this roll move with a soft rubber ball or a tennis ball. Work on it with one of your friends.

Slumps

All hitters at all levels have slumps. Once you have good fundamentals, do not make major changes. If you are in a slump, you are probably not doing the fundamentals properly. Stick with the fundamentals.

Watching the Pros

Some major league hitters do not have great mechanics. They have so much natural ability that they might even be successful for a while. Great hitters have solid mechanics. Major league hitters with different kinds of stances or movements at the plate are fun to imitate, but you should use your good fundamentals during your games.

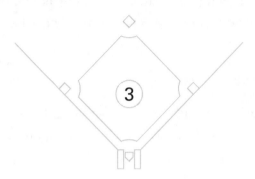

HITTING DRILLS

The drills in this chapter will help you develop and practice the good hitting fundamentals you learned in chapter 2.

Becoming a good hitter takes practice, lots of it. Even at the major league level players continually work on their swing mechanics. If you can be a good hitter with only a couple of rounds of batting practice at team practices, you are indeed gifted. Most good hitters must work hard on their skills to improve. They do a lot of this work on their own. You can also practice on your own in your backyard or at a park using the drills in this chapter. Some of the drills will require a partner. You can do some of them by yourself. You can do these drills with tennis balls, Wiffle balls, or real baseballs. If you will be using hardballs, wear a batting helmet. Take care to have a safe setup whenever and wherever you practice.

TEE DRILLS

Okay, you've already played T-ball and think it's only for the real little kids. In fact, the tee can be, and is, used for drills at all levels of baseball. One good thing about using the tee is that you can practice all by yourself. All you need is your bat, some balls, and the tee. If you don't have a tee, borrow one. Working with the tee is that important.

Find a place to practice where you will be hitting the ball into a solid backstop. You don't want to spend your valuable practice time chasing the ball. Again, if you are using hardballs, wear a helmet.

Hitting a baseball is a fast and continuous movement. We have divided this movement into two major parts to make it easier for you to develop specific skills.

Practicing Making Contact

Put a ball on the tee. Begin in your stance with the upright part of the tee just a little ahead of your front foot. Your feet should be set slightly wider apart than the

width of your shoulders. Bend slightly at your knees and waist. Your weight should be on the balls of your feet, and you should have about 60 percent of your weight on your back foot. Your feet should be parallel. Your hands and body should be relaxed. Your bat should be at a forty-five-degree angle to the ground. Your back elbow should be down but not touching your body. Keep your head still and focus your eyes on the ball. You must be balanced and your head must be still.

Take a short stride forward with your front foot. Bring your bat to the ready position. Start the swing

with your hands by moving them toward the pitcher. They should be near the middle of your chest. The bat knob should be pointed toward the pitcher, and the barrel of the bat should be pointed toward where the umpire stands.

Next, snap the bat to the contact position, stopping it at the ball. As you go to the contact position, roll up on the toe of your back foot and pivot your hips toward the pitcher. Your belly will be pointing toward the pitcher and a little more than half of your weight will now be on your front foot.

Go through these steps several times without taking a full swing to get the feel of the movements. When going through these movements you are building a muscle memory for good swing mechanics. Always keep your head still and maintain good balance. It is almost impossible to be a consistent hitter if either of these things is missing as you swing.

Practicing Completing the Swing

After you have practiced making contact several times and have a good feel for the process, take a full swing through the contact position. After you contact the ball, let your wrists roll through and let the bat follow through. Your eyes should see the bat contact the ball, and you should still be balanced through the swing and follow-through.

Good mechanics are the foundation of an efficient, tight, powerful swing. Anytime you feel a slip or variation that throws you off balance, go back to the tee and practice the parts.

PLAYING PEPPER

This drill is probably as old as baseball itself. It helps you learn to make good contact and develop good bat control. Usually, three or four players stand side by side about twenty feet in front of you. One lobs an underhand toss into your strike zone. You should stride and softly contact the ball. A tosser fields the ball and the drill continues until you miss or foul off three pitches. You now become a tosser. This drill can also be done with only one other person and can be done almost anywhere. It is a good pregame drill. It also works well to practice bunting.

THE FENCE DRILL

Good hitters have a quick, tight, compact swing. A big, loopy swing is a short trip to strikeouts. The fence drill is designed to help you tighten your swing. You can use any fence at the park. Face the fence, hold the knob end of the bat touching your stomach and move to where the other end of the bat is touching the fence. Take your batting stance. Go slowly through your stride and swing, stopping at the contact position. If you are moving your bat properly to the contact position, the bat won't touch the fence. Go through your swing to contact slowly several times, then increase your swing

speed and take several full swings to complete the drill. Your bat may barely tick the fence on some swings, but your swing will be tight.

THE BATTING STICK

Practicing on the tee is hitting a stationary ball. Now we get to a moving object. The stick is usually made of plastic or fiberglass with a handle on one end and something representing a ball on the other end. It takes two people to do a drill with the stick: a holder, and a hitter. The hitter sets up in a stance ready to hit. The holder is

facing the batter at a distance that will allow the ball on the stick to be moved through the batter's strike zone. The holder says "hit," then moves the ball into the strike zone and the batter strides and hits the ball on the end of the stick. This drill is good because you can get in a lot of swings without a need to retrieve the ball. Again, the mechanics of the full swing are exactly the same as you practiced in the tee drill.

SOFT TOSS

For soft toss you need two people and a fence or back-stop to hit toward. The tosser kneels, facing the batter,

at three or four bat lengths from the batter. The tosser should be about one step ahead of the batter's front foot. The batter sets up in the stance. The tosser says, "hit," and then tosses the ball. The toss should be a soft lob in the strike zone toward the batter's front hip. The batter strides and swings as the toss is made. Soft toss is good for practice with a friend and it also serves as a good pregame warm-up for hitters.

PITCHING MACHINES

Many youth leagues have a setup with a pitching machine and a batting cage. This is a good place to work on timing and swing mechanics. The person feeding the machine should hold up the ball, show it to the batter, then feed it into the machine. Stride and hit the ball. A machine is good in that the batter gets a lot of cuts at a moving ball, but the machine has some drawbacks. First, once the machine is properly adjusted, it will throw a strike on every pitch. The batter doesn't get to practice not swinging at bad pitches. Second, the machine will throw at a constant speed. Once a batter has the pitches timed, the machine should be easy to hit on almost every pitch. Pitching machines have a value, especially early in the season when hitters need a lot of swings, but they are not as good as live batting practice.

LIVE BATTING PRACTICE

This is normally part of regular team practices. Live batting practice takes more work than hitting in a cage because there must be a pitcher and players to shag balls, but it is worth the effort in batter development. Coaches or whoever else is pitching will not be able to throw perfect pitches. Batters can get good practice at taking bad pitches, and going after the ones in the strike

zone. The pitcher also won't be able to throw at a constant speed. This forces batters to adjust in order to time and hit each pitch. Finally, the batter gets practice at picking up the ball as it leaves the pitcher's hand in the delivery. Picking up the ball as early as possible is an important key to becoming a good hitter.

SCRIMMAGE GAMES

Your coach can set up different game situations with a scrimmage at practice. This is absolutely the best batting practice of all. Pitchers working batters in a game situation helps everyone on the team. You'll learn a lot about your hitting skill in a game situation batting against your team's pitching staff. Learn from the experience. It will give you key things to practice and improve.

DROP DRILL—ADVANCED

This drill is potentially dangerous. It should be done very carefully and with safety in mind. It starts like soft toss, with the batter set up to hit the ball into a net or fence. The person who will drop the ball *must be outside the arc of the bat when the batter swings*. The dropper will be slightly ahead of the batter's front foot so the ball will be dropped at the contact point. The dropper reaches out holding the ball above shoulder height. The

dropper says, "hit," and drops the ball down through the contact point. The batter strides and hits the ball as it drops. The main value of this drill is to help develop a quick swing and make the batter focus on and see the ball to hit it. Like the other drills it helps develop good hand-eye coordination.

BACK DOOR TOSS DRILL—ADVANCED

This drill sets up like the drop drill with the hitter and tosser facing a net or fence, except the tosser stands three or four bat lengths behind the batter. The tosser

says, "hit," and tosses a soft lob through the strike zone. The batter strides and hits the ball. This drill also helps develop concentration, a quick swing, and hand-eye coordination. It is a tough drill to master, but, as with the drop drill, a good hitter will make contact most of the time.

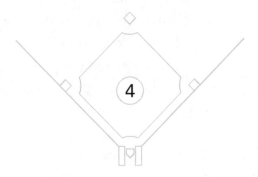

BUNTING FUNDAMENTALS

It's fun to hit away. Nothing looks better to a hitter than a solid line drive going into a gap in the outfield. However, to become a total offensive player, you also have to learn to bunt. Bunting is a basic fundamental skill that all batters should develop. Good hand-eye coordination is needed for hitting and the same goes for bunting. It's not as easy as it looks. Becoming a good bunter will take a lot of practice. In this chapter, you will learn to properly execute four different kinds of bunts.

THE SACRIFICE BUNT

This is the most basic bunt. The mechanics of a sacrifice bunt are the same for left-handed and right-handed batters. Position yourself near the front of the batter's box. Don't make the movement obvious because it may give away your intention. Moving to the front of the box gives you a better angle to reliably get the bunt down in fair territory as shown in the photo.

When the pitcher is in the windup, square around to bunt. This means you turn your body and both feet so you are facing the pitcher. Your knees should be bent slightly for good balance. Grasp the bat near the knob with your bottom hand. Next slide your top hand about halfway up the barrel of the bat, holding it between your thumb and your bent index finger. Be sure to keep

your thumb and fingers behind the bat to prevent the pitch from injuring them. Position the bat level to the ground in front of your body at about chest height and wait for the pitch.

The reason you start with the bat at chest level is because you want the bat movement to be downward toward the pitch. This increases your chances of getting the bunt on the ground. If you start with the bat lower and have to move it up to make contact, it increases the chances that you'll pop up the bunt.

As the pitch comes in, move your bat (keeping it level to the ground) into position to contact the ball. Don't move the bat forward toward the ball or peck at it. This punching movement can result in a weak ground ball in the infield. You want the fielders moving toward the plate as they pick up the ball and try to throw you out at first. Let the ball hit the bat as you hold it. Good bunters can "deaden the ball" by pulling the bat slightly back before contact. When the pitch solidly strikes the bat, the ball will jump out and quickly die after rolling a short distance on the ground. This sacrifice bunt will force the defense to make a play.

BUNTING FOR A HIT

Take a normal batting stance. Surprise is important here. As the pitcher releases the ball, quickly pivot on

your back foot with your belly facing the pitcher. This is similar to the basic contact position you learned in chapter 2. Slide your top hand up the bat, holding it the same way as you hold it for sacrifice bunts. Hold the bat at chest height as the pitch arrives. Your knees should be bent and your hands should be relaxed. You should be ready to run. Experiment with foot placement to find out the quickest way for you to get out of the batter's box. You should have a clear idea of where you want to place the bunt.

THE DRAG BUNT

Left-handed hitters have another tool available to them if they learn to drag bunt. This type of bunt is almost always used to try to get a base hit. These aren't for every player because they require very good hand-eye coordination, timing, and bat control. To execute this type of bunt, you open your right foot toward first base and are actually moving when the ball contacts the bat. You try to "drag" the ball to the right side of the infield with you as you are moving. The best drag bunts go past the pitcher and die on the infield grass. This is a good offensive tool if you can make it work.

THE FAKE BUNT

The fake bunt is primarily about strategy. When you do the fake bunt, you are really taking the pitch but you want to learn something about the other team's defense. To fake the bunt, square around exactly like you would for a sacrifice bunt. As the pitch comes in, jerk the bat back out of the strike zone. If you leave the bat near the strike zone, even a bad pitch may be called a strike because the umpire may think that you offered at it.

STAYING IN THE BATTER'S BOX TO BUNT

If you contact the ball with a foot on the ground outside of the batter's box, the umpire will likely call you out.

This will seldom happen when you are hitting away. It usually happens in bunt situations and you need to pay special attention to the batter's box when you bunt.

BUNTING PRACTICE DRILLS

Next are two basic drills that can improve your effectiveness in bunting.

The Glove Drill

This drill should help you get used to making contact. If you are a right-handed hitter, put your glove on your

right hand. If you are a left-handed hitter, put your glove on your left hand. Stand at the plate in your bunting position. Have someone throw medium-speed pitches over the plate. Reach out and let the ball hit the glove. Don't catch the ball. Just stop it with your glove. If you can consistently stop the pitches with your glove, you should be able to make consistent contact when you bunt.

The Placement Drill

The best bunts are usually down or near a baseline. Use your bottom hand to angle the bat to make the bunt go toward the first or third baseline. You can practice bunting almost anywhere. Lay out a string or something to represent baselines. Have someone toss the ball to you and practice placing ten hits in a row down each line. If you can do ten in a row down each line, you will have excellent bunt placement.

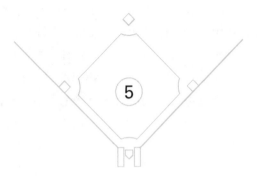

BEFORE YOU BAT

Are you ready to bat? That's a silly question. You're always ready to bat. After all, that's where you have the most fun in the game. You've had pregame batting practice and feel good. The following paragraphs give you some suggestions to help you prepare to have a good at bat. You should pay close attention to game situations when you are in the dugout or the on-deck circle. Try to pick up keys that might increase your odds of success. Being mentally prepared can eliminate some surprises and have you ready to make a good contribution to the team when your turn comes.

KNOW THE GAME SITUATION

Always be aware of the game situation. Know what inning you are in, the number of outs, where the runners are, and, of course, the score. Be prepared for what the coach may ask you to do. You should be ready to hit away, but there may be a situation with runners on base when you could expect a bunt signal. If there is a fast runner on first, your coach may put on a steal or a hit and run.

YOUR ON-DECK JOB

When you are the on-deck batter, you have a special responsibility in helping the runner when there may be a play at home plate. It is your job to tell the runner coming down the third baseline toward the plate whether or not to slide. On any play at the plate you should be positioned in back of the plate so the runner is coming directly at you. Stay far enough back from the plate area so you don't interfere with the play. If it is not a close play, hold your hands above your head and yell "stay up." On a close play, motion down with your hands and yell "get down" if you think the runner should slide.

STUDY THE PITCHER

In the dugout and on deck are good times to study the opposing pitcher. It is obvious whether the pitcher is right- or left-handed, but pitching motions vary a lot. Study the pitcher's motion. Know what to expect. The pitcher may have a smooth delivery or maybe one that is herky-jerky. See if the pitcher keeps the ball well hidden until the release. You will also need to watch where you will first see the ball when it is released. There is a lot of difference between the release point of a side-arm pitch and one that is overhand.

All pitchers are not in a good fielding position after their deliveries. When the delivery is finished, note how the pitcher follows through. Some pitchers fall to one side of the mound when they follow through. If the pitcher delivers the pitch and fades off the mound toward third base, he would be at a disadvantage trying to field a bunt or ground ball toward the right side of the infield. If he fades toward first, fielding balls toward the left side could be a problem.

Try to pick up on the pitcher's speed. This may be hard to tell from the sideline, but you can tell how other hitters on your team are dealing with the pitcher's fastball. Ask other team members what pitches they saw.

The pitches may be all fastballs or there may be change-ups or curveballs mixed in. Try to learn as much as you can about the pitcher's assortment. Look for a pattern in how the pitches are used. Some pitchers get into a rut. They don't work batters as much as they pitch according to the count. For example, see if there is a situation when the pitcher always throws a change-up.

For some reason, pitchers fall in love with a certain pitch and use it again and again in a given situation. One of the most common situations is trying to use a curveball as the strikeout pitch when the pitcher is way ahead in the count. If you see any pattern like this, you can be ready for the pitch.

WATCH THE COUNT

Pay attention to how deep in the count the other batters on your team are taking the pitcher. Walks, consistent 2–2 or 3–1 or full counts may signal a pitcher with a control problem. If the pitcher is struggling, you may be selective in the pitch you hit. If you don't help the pitcher by swinging at bad pitches, you may draw a base on balls. When some pitchers get behind in the count, they throw easier and just try to get the ball over the plate. Some pitchers want to get ahead in the count so badly that they'll throw a perfect strike on the first pitch almost every time. When the pitcher serves you a fat pitch, be ready and drive it somewhere.

LEFT-HANDED BATTERS

For some reason many young pitchers struggle when they face a left-handed batter. It may be because they don't see very many lefties or they don't practice pitching to a batter on that side of the plate. However, many lefties go to the plate and simply get very few pitches they can hit. If you are a lefty, be patient. Take what comes. Be ready to drive a fat pitch or take a walk if you have to. You get a chance to score either way.

RELAX

Okay, it's your turn. Go to the plate confident and relaxed. This pitcher is not going to fool you. Relieve any tension you feel with a couple of deep breaths. You're ready to hit.

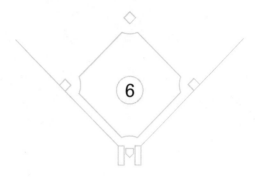

HITTING WITH A PURPOSE

When you step into the batter's box, you are stepping into some kind of hitting situation. Most of the time, your coach will decide what you are to do. The coach may want you to bunt, fake bunt, or even take a pitch. Your job is to execute what the coach wants you to do as well as possible.

HITTING AWAY

Many times you will come to the plate when your purpose is just to get on base. At other times, your main purpose is to drive in runs or advance runners by swinging away. If you are fast and think you can bunt for a hit, try it. However, most of the time you will be trying to hit the ball hard somewhere.

Making Consistent Contact

The best way to help your team is to hit consistent line drives. Do not try to hit home runs. The major problem with trying to hit home runs is that this causes young players to change their good mechanics. They usually get off balance and out of control; they lunge and try to uppercut the ball. If you are strong enough, some of your line drives will leave the park.

Hitting the Ball Where It's Pitched

A common saying in baseball is "Hit it where it's pitched." This saying means that you should pull the inside pitch and drive the outside pitch to the opposite field. Do it now if you can, but if you can't it's okay. This is very difficult even for major leaguers to do. You will have time to work on this as you get older.

As a young player, you should pay much more attention to hitting the center of the ball with the center of the bat. Let your eyes tell your hands where to go and you will naturally hit to all fields.

HITTING YOUR PITCH

Even if you are best friends, you and the pitcher are trying to use every advantage to accomplish your purposes. The pitcher is trying to upset your timing and get you out. The pitcher has a natural advantage because it is likely that the best hitters in your league will hit around .400. You are trying to get a hit, drive in a run, and score a run. You can increase your advantage by being smart about hitting.

Know the Strike Zone

The strike zone is a rectangle that goes from your armpits to your knees and covers the width of the plate. If you swing at a pitch outside of the strike zone, you are helping the pitcher. Many strikeouts at all levels come from swinging at bad pitches out of the strike zone. Start to pay attention to how often major league hitters strike out on bad pitches. You might be surprised at how often it happens.

For many young players, the high pitch looks very tempting. Young players probably strike out more often on the high pitch out of the strike zone than any other pitch. This does not need to happen. Remember, in your stance and ready positions, your hands are at the top of the strike zone. An easy way to lay off the high pitch is to not swing at anything over your hands.

Good pitchers will try to pitch you at the knees and over the outside part of the plate. These are the hardest pitches to hit. You can gain some advantage by knowing exactly where the low strike is and not swinging at pitches at your ankles and in the dirt.

One very good technique to help you in hitting strikes is called "the hitting window." Visualize the rectangular strike zone as a window in front of the plate. As the ball starts to pass through the "window," rip it.

Know the Count

Keep your head in the game. Knowing the count can help you gain an advantage over the pitcher. Most young pitchers will start a batter with a fastball and throw a fastball most of the time, even if they can throw a change-up or a curveball. Pitchers are usually taught to throw fastballs until they get ahead in the count. This fact can help you as a hitter. Always look for fastballs and adjust to other pitches.

- ◆ Be a first-ball, fastball hitter. The pitcher will try to get ahead of you. Be ready to get a good rip at the first pitch.

- If you are ahead in the count, you will almost always see a fastball.

- If you are behind in the count, it is important that you do not look for a curve or a change-up. If you do, a fast pitcher can throw one by you. Remember, look for the fastball and adjust.

- Most young pitchers do not throw anything but a fastball until they have two strikes on a batter. They will then use a curveball or a change-up.

The 2–0, 3–0, and 3–1 counts give the batter a special advantage. In most cases the coach will have you taking on 3–0. Take a good look at that pitch. It will be a fastball and you will see it again. The same goes for 2–0 and 3–1 counts. These are the hitter's pitches. You will see a fastball on these pitches. Pick a pitch you can drive. Look for a fastball down the middle, belt high. This is called "zoning the pitch." If the pitcher does not give you your pitch, let it go. The next pitch will be another fastball.

Hitting with Two Strikes

You should make a few basic adjustments to your hitting approach when you have two strikes. With two strikes, your main purpose is to get the ball in play.

- Protect the plate. You do not want to be called out on strikes. If the pitch is close enough for an umpire to call a strike, swing at it. If it's too close to take, don't take it. Be an aggressive two-strike hitter.

- Move forward in the batter's box and choke up on the bat. These two adjustments will put you in a better position to hit the ball in front of the plate and give you better bat control. You are still looking for a fastball, but you will be able to adjust better to a two-strike curveball or change-up from this position.

- Some hitters move their hands forward to the middle of their chests and slightly open up their front shoulders with two strikes. Experiment and see if you can do this. It will allow you to "slap" the ball through the infield.

Bunting for a Base Hit

If you can bunt and have good speed, you may be able to bunt for base hits. Use the bunting technique you learned in chapter 4. To be able to surprise the defense, you can't give your intent to bunt until the pitcher has almost released the ball. If the first and third basemen are playing deep, a bunt about twenty feet down the first or third baselines can result in a single. Another good approach is to try to "push the ball past the pitcher" toward either the shortstop or the second baseman. Right-handed pitchers tend to finish their deliveries more toward first base. So against right-handers, try to push the ball toward the shortstop. Against left-handers, try to push the ball toward the second baseman.

Being a Switch Hitter

In one way or another, this chapter has talked about getting an advantage over the pitcher. One of the biggest advantages you can have as a hitter is to be able to hit from both sides of the plate. It is not as important to young players as older players. Put simply, you get a better look at the ball and it's easier to hit good breaking pitches coming to you than going away from you.

The advantage of left-handed hitters against right-handed pitchers and vice versa is well established. Most major league teams platoon players in the starting lineup for that reason. As you watch the pros, you will see many pitching changes at the end of the game as managers try to gain the natural advantage.

Try hard to be a switch hitter. Being a good switch hitter can keep you in the game and make you a better hitter.

RUNNING THE BASES

There are only eighteen outs allowed your team's offense in a regulation game. It is a gift to the defense if your team gives up outs by making baserunning errors. Smart baserunning can win ball games. It is a critical component of total offensive play. In games at your age group, a runner who reaches second base with less than two outs scores a high percentage of the time. Blinding speed is helpful, but it can seldom fully substitute for being a smart, heady base runner. In this chapter we will cover different situations and how a base runner should react. Watch and listen for your base coach. In most cases the base coach will be directing you with voice and/or hand signals.

ROUNDING THE BASES

Now you're the batter and you've hit the ball to the out-field. Run to first, touch the inside edge of the bag with your right foot and round first like you are going to second. If it's a base hit and the coach holds you up, take the turn and return to first. If the ball is caught, pull up and go to the dugout. Look at and listen to your coach. If the coach tells you to go, get to second as fast as you can. Before getting to second, look to your third-base coach. The third-base coach should be giving a signal and telling you to hold up, slide, or continue coming

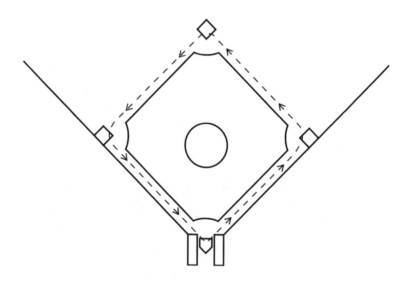

toward third. As you near third base, the coach may tell you to hold up, slide, or go. If the signal is to go, head toward home and look for a signal to stand up or slide from the on-deck batter.

As you run the bases, you should make a short loop to the right as you approach the base. This loop lets you run straight in the base path to the next base. The fastest path going from first around second base to third or second around third to home will be rounding the bases, touching each on the inside corner with the right foot.

RUN THROUGH FIRST BASE

Now you have hit a ground ball to the infield and are running toward first base. This may sound silly, but you must run *all* the way to first as hard as you can. Stay between the double lines that start near first base. Drive through the base and don't let up until *after* you have crossed the bag. It is a common fault of runners to either hesitate before reaching the bag or make a leap at the bag. Either action gives extra time for the defense to get you out. After you've crossed the bag, turn to the right into foul territory. If you were safe at first and turn into fair territory, this indicates that you are attempting to advance to second and you may be tagged out.

ON BASE

When you are on base, keep your head in the game. Always know the count on the batter and the number of outs. As you will see, outs and the count can trigger some automatic responses by base runners. If you are not sure about the count or outs, ask your base coach or the base umpire.

At your age group, runners can't lead off before the pitch. That will come when you reach the next level. However, when you are on any base, get into the sprinter's stance with your back foot ready to push off the base. When the pitch crosses the plate, take a couple of quick steps toward the next base. You want to get

a little head start in case you need to run. There are a lot of passed balls and wild pitches at this level. You should be ready to run on each pitch. Don't go so far off base that you can be picked off by a catcher's throw. The coach should tell you to get back if the catcher throws. *Don't take your eyes off of the ball,* and go immediately back to the base if the situation does not require you to run.

If you let a batted ball touch you when you are in fair territory, you will usually automatically be called out. When you are the runner on third base, take your leadoff steps on the foul-ball side of the baseline. If a batted ball strikes you in foul territory, you are not out. It is only a foul ball.

TAGGING UP

You are the runner on third base. There are less than two outs and the batter has hit a fly ball to the outfield. The third-base coach tells you to tag up. Get to the base and get into your sprinter's stance facing home plate. When the outfielder catches the ball, the coach should tell you to go! Break for the plate as soon as you hear "go." As you are heading down the line, look for the on-deck batter beyond home plate. The on-deck batter should be there to tell you to either stand up or slide.

If the fly ball is not hit deep into the field, the coach may have you fake going to home to draw a throw. Take three or four running steps toward the plate, then stop and return to third. If you do draw a bad throw and the ball gets away from a fielder, you may be able to score. The coach must make the decision to send you.

You are on second base again with less than two outs. A fly ball is hit toward deep right field. The third-base coach may want you to tag up and advance to third after the catch. This may happen when the coach believes the outfielder has a weak arm. Go to the base, get set, and start on "go." Watch the coach for a stand-up or slide signal as you near third base. Tagging up at first base to advance on a fly ball is a very low percentage play because second base is too close to all outfield positions.

HALFWAY

Now you are on first base and there are less than two outs. A fly ball is hit to right field. Go a little less than halfway toward second base and return to first base immediately if the ball is caught. Do not go far enough to be doubled off after the catch. If the fielder misses the ball, you should be able to easily get to second base or maybe to third if the coach waves you on.

Next, you are on second base with less than two outs. The fly ball is hit to the outfield, and the coach has not told you to tag up. Go about halfway to third. The coach may send you home to score if the ball is mis-played. Again, if the ball is caught, don't get doubled off.

WHEN TO RUN

You will always run with the pitch when there are two outs and there is a full count on the batter if: 1) You are on first base; or 2) You are on second and there is a runner on first; or 3) You are on third base and the bases are loaded. You will always run with two outs when a batter hits the ball.

You will usually run when you are on first or second if a passed ball or wild pitch gets by the catcher to the backstop. When you are on third base, run to score on a passed ball or wild pitch only when the coach sends you.

You must run on an infield ground ball when you may be forced at the next base. One caution: when you are on first base with less than two outs and the batter hits an infield grounder, you must advance toward second. As soon as the fielder catches the ball at second to start a double play, slide, no matter how far you are from second base. The relay throw to first to complete a double play will pass very close to your head. Getting down with a slide can prevent a potentially serious injury.

STEALING BASES

The coach should decide steal attempts. A steal signal will be given to you by a base coach or from the dugout.

You can't lead off, so stealing on the pitcher's motion will need to wait for later years. If you are fast, you may be able to steal second base or maybe even third on a catcher with a weak arm. If you get a steal signal, set up ready to go when the pitch crosses the plate and be prepared to slide when you reach the base.

Watch for a steal signal when there are runners on first and third with less than two outs. Many teams will simply concede the steal without a play at second. A few teams will risk giving up a run to go after the runner stealing second. Beyond this, first and third steal defenses vary widely. Some teams automatically throw directly to third to try to pick off the runner. The throw may go back to the pitcher who then tries to make a play on the runner at third. Others try some type of trick fake throw play to pick the runner off third base. There are other variations, but few will ever work when the runner at third holds close to the base and stays alert.

SLIDE!

Executing a good slide to avoid a tag on a close play at a base can really help your team. Your mother or whoever else does your laundry isn't going to like this, but good sliding takes practice. You're going to get dirty. To prevent injuries, find a sandy or loose dirt area to practice. Set up something to serve as a base and practice.

Hook

You will be sliding on one of your hips when you do a hook slide and on both hips and your back when you do a straight-in slide. Wearing sliding pads will help prevent injuries in games as well as when you practice. Please do not practice or try sliding headfirst like Pete Rose. You may be seriously injured if you collide with a fielder's feet or legs or the base itself.

To practice, measure off a distance of about sixty feet from your base. Practice getting a good fast start toward the base, sprint, and slide into the base. At first it is hard to judge how far from the base to start your slide. You want to reach the base, but not slide over or

Straight

past it. With practice you will soon learn how to make it just right. It is good to use a flat object as your base, so that you don't jam and injure your foot or leg if you overslide. Practice hook slides to both the right and left side of the base. Also practice a straight-in slide.

Keep your head in the game, be alert, and listen to your coaches. You don't need to be the fastest player on the team to be a very good base runner.

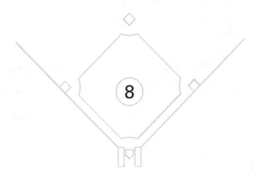

ADVANCING BASE RUNNERS

The ability to advance runners and force the defense to make plays is essential to quality team offense. After all, the purpose of team offense is to score runs. In this chapter, we will cover good, proven strategies for advancing runners.

THE BUNT

Executed properly, a bunt in the right situation can be a powerful offensive weapon. In an age that glorifies home runs, a simple ten-foot bunt down a baseline can be the key to winning a game. Bunt strategy will almost always be decided on and signaled by your coach.

However, it is important for you to know these situations so that you can execute properly.

The Fake Bunt

If your coach has not scouted the other team, a fake bunt is a good way to learn how they will defense the bunt. You know how to fake bunt. Your coach should have a signal for it and wants to see what happens when you do it. You should square around early as if you are going to bunt and pull the bat back out of the strike zone well before the pitch arrives at the plate. Pay attention to which infielders charge the plate when you fake bunt. The defense should commit. The actions of the first and third basemen will usually give away the other team's bunt coverage.

The fake bunt can accomplish other things. First, it can be a threat to a defense that is not very good at making plays on bunts. It makes them think. The first and third basemen may move in a few steps toward the plate, and make it easier to hit the ball past either position. A fake bunt might also distract a pitcher or catcher and cause a wild pitch or passed ball.

The Sacrifice Bunt

With a runner on first base or runners on first and second, your coach may signal a sacrifice bunt. A runner in scoring position (on second or third) with less than two outs will score a high percentage of the time. When asking for a sacrifice bunt, the coach is willing to give up an out to advance a runner or runners into better scoring positions.

When the pitcher is in the delivery, square around and use the sacrifice bunting method you learned in chapter 4. Make sure you get the bunt down. A pop-up bunt in this situation can result in an easy double play. At a minimum, the sacrifice bunt should result in runners advancing and you being thrown out at first. Successful sacrifice bunts do not count against your batting average.

The sacrifice bunt does another important thing. It forces the defense to make a play. A team always helps itself when it forces the defense to make a play. Other than advancing runners, there are numerous ways a sacrifice bunt can work in your favor. The bunt may be so good that you beat it out for a hit. It may be misplayed by a fielder or the fielder may make a bad throw. A poor defensive play on a bunt can result in runs being scored.

The Squeeze Play

The squeeze play is used when there is a runner on third base with less than two outs. When signaling for a squeeze bunt, the coach is usually willing to give up an out to try to score a run. The squeeze bunt is commonly used as a surprise tactic. It works as a sacrifice bunt on the part of the batter. When you contact the ball, the runner at third should break for home and try to score before a play can be made at the plate. Another way to execute the squeeze play is for the runner at third to come off the base and try to score as the play is made on the runner at first. Because young players under twelve years old can't lead off at third base, this is not a high percentage play. It works best when there is a good bunter at the plate and a fast runner at third.

BEATING THE BASIC BUNT DEFENSES

Your coach will usually give you the sacrifice bunt sign with a runner on first or runners on first and second with no outs or one out. Your job is to make the play work as well as possible. Knowing how the other team defenses the bunt is important.

There are three basic bunt defenses with runners on first or first and second. The second baseman and the shortstop have roles to play, but they have nothing to do with where you bunt the ball. You should pay close attention to the first and third baseman and the pitcher.

1. The third baseman charges. The first baseman stays at first base. The pitcher covers the first baseline.
2. The first baseman charges. The third baseman stays at third base. The pitcher covers the third baseline.
3. The first baseman, third baseman, and pitcher all charge.

The key to good execution of a sacrifice bunt is to bunt away from the charging fielder. So for defense 1, you should bunt down the first baseline. For defense 2, you should bunt down the third baseline. For defense 3, try to place the ball ten to fifteen feet in front of the plate. This defense is the most aggressive, but because so many players are moving around, you can be effective by bunting straight in front of you.

In very rare situations, the pitcher will cover all bunts. This means that the first and third baselines will both be good places to place the ball. If a team uses this kind of bunt defense, a good coach will usually bunt until the defense proves that it can make a play.

THE BATTER AND THE BASE STEALER

The stolen base is an obvious way to advance runners. The batter is not just an observer in steal situations.

Depending upon the situation, the batter and the base stealer have different roles to play.

The Straight Steal

You have speed on the bases, and your coach sees a chance to steal. Because it is a straight steal, you should take the pitch. However, you should stride toward the pitcher like you are going to hit, but keep your hands back. This movement may distract the catcher for an instant and help the runner.

The Hit and Run

Young players twelve years old and younger are not allowed to lead off. They cannot start the steal until the ball crosses the plate. Therefore, the hit and run for young players is a straight steal where your job is to hit away. The coach wants you to swing the bat and get a hit. However, since you need to protect the runner, you should swing at the pitch regardless of where it is thrown. If the pitch is way outside, do not step on the plate. If you make contact with the ball, the umpire will call you out.

The Fake Bunt and Steal

Your role in the fake bunt and steal is to get the defense moving around. You should try to convince the other team that you are actually going to bunt. Move to your regular sacrifice bunt position and pull the bat back as the ball approaches the plate. The catcher might be distracted and the movement of defensive players may cause a base coverage mistake or throwing error.

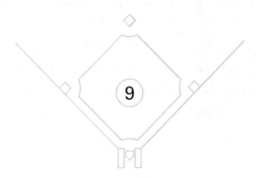

TEAM OFFENSE

A team is not just a collection of individuals. On a good offensive baseball team, each player has several roles to play to help the team. When all players get the job done, good things happen. Good hitting, bunting, and baserunning create action and excitement. It is a lot of fun to be a part of that.

CHARACTERISTICS OF GOOD OFFENSIVE TEAMS

Good offensive teams have some major characteristics in common.

♦ They put pressure on the defense and not on themselves. The players are confident that they can execute what they are asked to do.

- Hitters are aggressive at the plate. They are not looking for walks. They swing the bat. They place bunts where they should be.
- Base runners are aggressive on the bases. It is a basic fact that the ability to run develops before the abilities to anticipate a play or field a ball and throw it accurately. Good young teams will force the defense to throw them out.
- Good offensive teams hit strikes. They do not help the pitcher by swinging at bad pitches. Most of all, they do not take a two-strike pitch that is "too close to take."
- All players know their roles. They do not try to do more than they can, but they do what they can well.
- Players know that good offense comes from everyone contributing. They think about starting and keeping rallies alive. They know that no one hitter or base runner, no matter how good, can create enough offense to consistently win games.
- Players in the lineup "pick each other up." This common baseball expression is based upon the idea that if one player is not successful, another will do well in order to keep the offense going.

- Players are contact hitters and do not "swing from the heels" trying to hit home runs.
- Players always have their heads in the game. They understand the situation. They are ready to properly execute. They do not make mental errors and do not miss the coach's signs.

YOUR ROLE IN THE BATTING ORDER

Batting orders are not put together by accident. They are designed to make the best use of the abilities of all players. Most coaches arrange the batting order in the following way:

The Top of the Order

The first three hitters in the batting order are usually among the best athletes on the team. They are bunched together early in the order so that they can bat more often. Their overall role is to "set the table" for the middle of the batting order. However, each player has a role to play:

- The leadoff hitters: these players are usually very fast and have a good batting eye. They get the ball in play and are good bunters and base runners. Their main role is to get on base. Many times, these players are left-handed batters, because pitchers are not as used to pitching to left-handed batters as they are to right-handed batters. Left-handed batters also start closer to first base.

- ◆ Number two hitters: these players are especially good at handling the bat. They are excellent bunters. They have a good eye and good speed. Their main roles are to get on base and advance runners.
- ◆ Number three hitters: the players with the highest batting average will usually bat third in the batting order. These players are very good athletes who have quick hands at the plate. They usually hit the ball hard somewhere. They are not asked to bunt very often. Their main role is to hit away.

The Middle Part of the Order

The number four, five, and six hitters are especially important to overall team offense. If the middle of the order is strong, a team can continue to put pressure on the defense and score more runs. Their overall role is to "clean the table" by driving in runs as well as getting on base.

- ◆ Number four hitters: clean-up hitters are usually stronger and have more power than other hitters. Their main role is to drive in the top three hitters.

- Number five hitters: these are good hitters who have less power than number four hitters and not as high a batting average as number three hitters. They must be versatile. Their main roles are to drive in runs, get a hit to keep a rally going, and advance runners.
- Number six hitters: these hitters are "your next-best hitters." These are still good hitters, but do not have the power or hit for the average that the number five hitters do. Their major roles are the same as the number five hitters.

The Bottom of the Order

For regular league teams, the hitters in the number seven, eight, and nine positions in the order are usually younger or do not hit as well as hitters in the top six positions. The reality is that, in most cases, these players play the minimum number of innings required by the league. They may only bat once a game. For all-star or select teams, the description above may not be true. Regardless, the hitters at the bottom of the order will be weaker hitters.

- Number seven, eight, and nine hitters: in order to help the team as much as possible, these players should use the good hitting techniques described in this book. The main role of these players is to get on base and advance base runners. They should make contact, think about getting the ball in play, and lay off bad pitches. They should try to bunt for hits, become good bunters, and be smart on the bases.

KEEPING A POSITIVE ATTITUDE

Sometimes you will not be able to execute as well as you desire. That is okay. Hitting is not always easy. After all, there are nine defensive players trying to get you out. The good thing is that you can always hit again. Stay positive.

Team offense is about the team. Team players do not enjoy being around players who sulk, throw things, or gripe on the bench. Pull for your teammates and they will pull for you. Good things will happen when teams have a positive attitude.

We have coached in situations where a big, strong pitcher might seem invincible. Then something happens. Maybe a fielder makes an error. Maybe someone rolls a ball through the infield. Maybe there is a walk or stolen base. Maybe it is something that someone says on the bench. What happens next is the best part of good offensive baseball. Your team "catches on fire." Every player knows that he can hit. There are line drives going all over the park. Runners are flying around the bases, and runs are being scored. It's a great feeling and great fun to be a part of that.

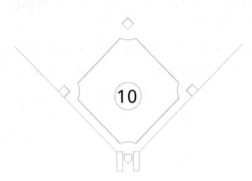

THE HITTER'S ATTITUDE

There is one final critical element that will separate you as a really good hitter from other batters. What goes on in the body part between your ears is a difference that will set you apart—the critical element is your attitude.

Throughout this book we have dealt extensively with batting mechanics. Following the instructions in the chapter on how to set up and make a swing will help you develop an efficient, powerful swing. The drills help you use these mechanics to build a sound muscle memory that kicks in as you go through the hitting process. The more you practice, the more efficient you will become, until setting up and making a good swing is an action requiring very little thought. It will be almost automatic.

Having read the chapters on strategy, such as advancing runners, bunting, and stealing bases, you have gained an understand of game situations and how to make a contribution to team success. You have developed an effective, powerful swing using sound mechanics. Now, your attitude, self-control, and concentration can determine how well you use these tools to be a successful hitter.

STAY POSITIVE

You must have a positive attitude at all times. Your objective in most at bats is to get a base hit. It's not easy, but you need to stay in a positive frame of mind even though you know that you'll be successful only three or four times out of each ten at bats. It would be easy to let bad at bats affect your attitude. Trust your swing and stay positive. You need to put disappointments behind you, knowing you'll get the job done next time around.

BE CONFIDENT

Good hitters are confident. They feel that they can make contact on any pitch in the strike zone. Once a good hitter has sized up a pitcher and looked at a pitch or two, he will believe he has an edge. He knows the strike zone. The good hitter can be fooled on a pitch. He logs it into memory, then concentrates on hitting the next pitch, knowing that the pitcher won't get by with that again. There isn't any reason here to repeat the part on hitting with a purpose or working the count. It's the pitcher's job to throw strikes. The confident batter knows that it only takes one pitch. When the good pitch comes he will drive it somewhere.

There is a thin line between being confident and becoming cocky. Success can bring on a cocky attitude. A cocky batter can become so overconfident and aggressive that his positive attitude becomes self-defeating. Confident hitters stay within themselves, use their sound mechanics, and keep each at bat in perspective.

DEALING WITH PRESSURE

Good hitters can deal with pressure. You're at bat. The game is on the line in the late innings. There are runners on base. Fans are going wild on both sides of the field, and your coach is having anxious fits in the dugout. You are the one who must remain calm and positive. You know that stress and tension can make it difficult for you to do your best. We've already told you how to deal with tension. Again, when you start to feel tense, step out of the batter's box and take a couple of deep breaths to calm yourself. The pitcher facing you is also certainly subject to the same stress of the situation. He must throw strikes, which is exactly what you want.

This is a situation calling for you to be cool and concentrate on your job. Don't let the pressure of the game lead you to abandon your sound mechanics. Concentrate on making a good swing. Think contact first. You can never go too far wrong by putting the ball into play. This puts pressure on the other team's defense. They must make a play.

Think positive, maybe you'll drill a shot into an outfield gap and clear the bases. Or, a ball you hit may be misplayed by the defense. If the pitcher starts to lose it, you may draw a walk. Don't ever be too proud to take a base on balls. You are a good hitter. You won't help the pitcher by chasing pitches out of the strike zone in this or any other less stressful situation.

BELIEVE IN YOURSELF

You have worked hard to develop a good, quick, compact, powerful swing. Stay with it and it will serve you well. A positive, businesslike "can-do" attitude combines with the physical part, leading to success as a hitter. Believe in your abilities, you will be successful.

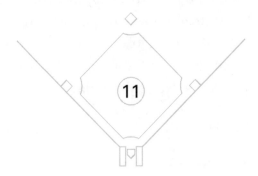

COMMON BATTING FAULTS

Much of this book is aimed at helping you to develop good, sound hitting mechanics. These points are presented in a positive, how-to manner. With practice and concentration you can develop and maintain good mechanics. But, during the course of a season some hitters start to lose their effectiveness because they change their mechanics or their approach to hitting. Some of these changes are made consciously, others happen without the player really being aware of them.

In the following discussion, we will describe some of the ways batters stray from sound mechanics, resulting in a loss of hitting effectiveness. A player's set-up and swing mechanics in the batter's box should be measured against the points in the chapter on hitting fundamentals. A teammate, coach, or parent may be able to spot changes and offer help. Once recognized, solutions to negative attitudes and approaches towards hitting problems are best solved by the player.

LOSS OF CONFIDENCE

If you don't believe you can hit a pitcher, you're doomed the instant you step into the batter's box. Perhaps you've seen the pitcher strike out the good hitters on your club or you think he's throwing so hard you just can't make contact with the pitches. Choke up, be aggressive, and trust your swing. The pitch must come through the strike zone. Think positive, you can hit this guy.

HOME RUN COMPLEX

It is hard to believe, but a home run can sometimes create real problems. Say a batter with a good, tight, compact swing makes solid contact and the ball clears the fence. Players, coaches, and fans make a big deal out of a home run. But keeping a home run in perspective is very important. If the player maintains sound mechanics and a positive approach to hitting, he should continue to be a good hitter.

On the other hand, a player who decides to go for the league title can make changes that create problems. Following are things many young players do to try to hit the ball harder, but which actually lead to strike-outs. All of these are easy to spot but not so easy to fix until the player changes his approach and objective toward hitting.

- Overswinging—Swing hard to hit the long ball, right? Wrong! Overswinging throws the batter off balance, making it very difficult to make solid contact. A solid foundation and good balance are necessary to hit consistently.
- Overstriding or lunging—This is similar to overswinging and maybe precedes a big hard swing. Overstriding and/or lunging robs a batter of power and adversely affects balance.
- Foot in the bucket—This is a term for a batter who strides down the baseline on the swing, attempting to pull the ball. Granted, once in a while a pull hitter will hit the long ball, providing the pitch is inside and about belt high. Smart pitchers work these pull hitters on the outside corner of the plate. These pitches to a batter putting a foot in the bucket usually result in a ground ball to the middle of the infield. Batters striding down the line also

strike out a lot. Your stride should always be short and toward the pitcher.

♦ Swinging up—This is sometimes done by wannabe home run hitters trying to lift the ball out of the yard. Abandoning a good level swing is a short road to striking out.

Before we go on, let's put the youth league home run in perspective. It is important for young players to learn and practice sound fundamentals. This is development for the future. Baseball plays a sort of dirty trick on young players. Until a player is twelve years old, he plays on a small field. The distance to the fences is about two hundred feet. At age thirteen everything on the field grows by at least 50 percent. Base length goes from sixty to ninety feet, and the fences are moved to three hundred feet or more.

So, the glorious high fly home run at age twelve will be a soft fly ball to deep shortstop or shallow left field the next year. The line drive homer at age twelve might be a base hit the next year, but probably not for extra bases. Of course, a player grows some in that transition year, but few if any grow 50 percent in either size or ability. It is better that the young player concentrate on sound principles of hitting. These will serve him best throughout his baseball career.

Next we will list other swing attributes that should be corrected. For reference or to answer questions, go back to the chapter on The Fundamentals of Hitting.

THE SET UP

- Foot placement—Setting up with the feet too close together, less than shoulder width apart, invites lunging and an off-balance swing. If the feet are set up too far apart, you are robbed of power and again your balance may be affected.
- Hands too high—Many young players try to copy major league batters who start their set-up with their hands way above their shoulder. If you watch closely, most of them move to the ready position you learned in the chapter The Fundamentals of Hitting before they start their swing. Trying to initiate your swing from a high-hands position affects the swing arc. The bat also must travel farther to reach the contact position, resulting in a slower swing.
- Bat not in the ready position—Again, copying another player's setup can become a problem. Refer to the chapter on fundamentals.
- Too far from the plate—Some batters set up so far from the plate that they cannot reach a pitch

on the outside half. This may be a symptom of a batter afraid of being hit by a pitch. The batter needs at least to be able to reach the outside part of the plate.

OTHER PROBLEMS

Following are some additional problems that are easy to see.

- Chasing bad pitches — You should be an aggressive hitter but you must also have the discipline to lay off pitches that are out of the strike zone.
- Head not solid — Good hitters see the bat contact the ball. There is a saying that where the head goes, so goes the body. Pulling your head and taking your eyes off of the ball makes it nearly impossible to make solid contact with any degree of consistency.
- Bat too heavy — This is self-explanatory. A player might hit a real slow pitcher with a bat that is too heavy, but the batter's balance will probably be affected. However, the player with an extra-heavy bat will seldom make contact on a fast pitcher.
- Loopy swing — This is something to avoid, it is the exact opposite of the tight, compact swing that we teach. A loopy swinger usually has his

arms extended from the beginning of the swing. Loopy swings are generally slow and have difficulty making solid contact on any pitch on the inside half of the plate. A wide loopy swing may also be caused by a bat that is too heavy.

To correct any of the above problems with mechanics, go back to the fundamentals and practice the drills to get back into your groove as a good, consistent contact hitter. The changes that are linked to attitude can possibly be corrected by this reminder:

You are part of a team, not a one-player show. You can best contribute to your team's success by being a consistent contact hitter.

ABOUT THE AUTHORS

Don Oster is a longtime baseball coach and current Indiana high school baseball and softball umpire. His Babe Ruth League team, for which he was the pitching coach, appeared in four consecutive World Series. He is also the author of *Largemouth Bass,* and the coauthor of *A Guide for Young Pitchers, A Guide for Young Softball Pitchers,* and *Hunting Today's Whitetail.* He lives in southern Indiana.

Bill McMillan has twenty years' experience coaching youth baseball as a manager and a pitching coach. His teams have won nine league championships and a Minnesota State Little League championship. He has served as a pitching coach for youth aged nine to sixteen. He has been a public school teacher and a university professor. He holds a PhD in educational psychology and has worked extensively at the state and national levels on various educational programs.